creatures
of the sea

Moray Eels

Other titles in the series:

Humpback Whales

The Octopus

Rays

Sea Stars

creatures of the sea

Moray Eels

Kris Hirschmann

KIDHAVEN
PRESS™

THOMSON
GALE™

San Diego • Detroit • New York • San Francisco • Cleveland
New Haven, Conn. • Waterville, Maine • London • Munich

LIBRARY OF CONGRESS CATALOGING-IN-PUBLICATION DATA

Hirschmann, Kris, 1967–
  Moray eels / by Kris Hirschmann.
    p. cm.—(Creatures of the sea)
  Includes bibliographical references.
  Summary: Examines the reef environment, life cycle, reputation, facts, and fiction of the moray eel.
    ISBN 0-7377-0985-5 (hardback : alk. paper)
  1.Morays—Juvenile literature. [1. Morays 2. Eels.] I. Title. II. Series.
  QL638 .M875 H57 2003
  597' .43—dc21

                                                                2002003261

Table of Contents

Introduction

Hidden Reef Dwellers

Coral reefs are full of life. A diver or a snorkeler who visits a coral reef can expect to see brightly colored fish darting back and forth, lobsters waving their long antennae, and sea stars inching their way across the ocean floor. Soft corals and sea grasses sway in the currents; crabs crawl to and fro; shrimp and other shellfish dot the reef. Color and movement are everywhere.

Amidst all this motion, still creatures such as moray eels are easy to miss. If a human visitor moves slowly and looks carefully, he or she may spot a moray eel resting under a rocky ledge or sticking out of a hole in the reef. A fast swimmer, however, will probably pass a moray without ever seeing it. The moray's stillness helps this reef dweller blend into the background.

A moray eel slithers between two rocks to explore its surroundings.

Many people assume that if morays are hard to spot in a certain area, there are not many of them around. But this is not the case. Coral reefs are full of moray eels. In one study, scientists squirted a mild poison into a reef's many cracks and holes. When the animals hiding in the reef came into the open water, the scientists discovered that there were many moray eels in the area. In fact, morays made up a large percentage of the animals on the reef. Not every reef has been studied in this way, but scientists are confident that morays are just as common in other areas.

Tracking Morays

Although morays are very common, they are not as well understood as many other ocean animals. Morays are shy and secretive creatures. This makes them hard to study. In the past decade, however, scientists have found a new way to study moray eels. They attach tiny electronic devices to morays and then use computers to track the eels' movements. This method has already helped scientists to learn a lot about the day-to-day lives of moray eels. As the years go by and information continues to be collected, more and more will be known about these interesting creatures of the sea.

1

Homes, Bodies, Habits

M oray eels belong to the **Anguilliformes** order, which also includes many other types of eels. In all, this order contains about 450 species of eels. Of these, about 125 are morays.

Moray Basics

Moray eels are warm-water creatures. They are found mostly in the tropical and subtropical coastal waters of the Indian, Pacific, and Atlantic Oceans. The freshwater moray eel and a few other types of morays live in rivers, lakes, and other freshwater bodies. But these species are not nearly as common as the saltwater varieties.

In their ocean homes, morays prefer coral reefs and rocky areas. These places are full of cracks and holes that provide plenty of hiding places. Morays also prefer shallow waters and are usually found at depths between 10 and 50 feet. (Morays are sometimes found as deep as 150 feet, but this is not common.)

Moray eels come in many different sizes. The smallest member of the family is the pygmy moray, which may measure as little as eight inches from its nose to tail tip. The largest of the morays, including the longtail and giant morays, may be more than ten feet long. Very short or very long morays are rare, however. Most morays fall somewhere in the middle of the range, measuring about four to five feet from end to end.

Within the moray family, there is a wide range of skin coloring and patterns. Some of these animals,

A large yellow moray eel greets a scuba diver in the remains of a sunken ship.

like the green moray, are one solid color all over. Others, like the black-and-white zebra moray, have striped skin. Still others are covered with colorful spots or blotches.

An Unusual Body

Moray eels are fish, but their bodies do not look like most fish. Long and slender, morays look more like underwater snakes than fish. A moray's body is not round like a snake's, though. It is squeezed inward on both sides, making the body oval rather than round.

A moray's fins are unusual too. Most fish have pectoral and ventral, or side, fins; dorsal, or back, fins; and anal, or stomach, fins that they use to steady themselves as they swim. They also have caudal, or tail, fins that push their bodies through the water. Moray eels do not have side fins or a distinct caudal fin. They do, however, have long dorsal and anal fins that run all the way down the body and meet at the tail tip. The dorsal fin usually starts right behind the moray's head; the anal fin starts about halfway down the belly. When a moray wiggles its body, these fins catch the water and help the eel to swim.

The moray's skin is also unusual. The bodies of most fish are covered in scales. But moray eels have no scales. Instead, they have tough skin that is coated with a thick layer of slime. The slime protects the eel from scrapes and other injuries.

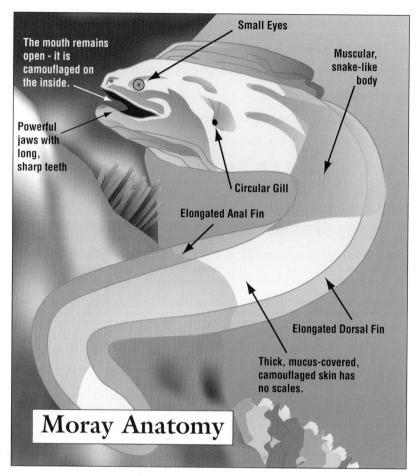

Small Eyes

The mouth remains open - it is camouflaged on the inside.

Muscular, snake-like body

Powerful jaws with long, sharp teeth

Circular Gill

Elongated Anal Fin

Elongated Dorsal Fin

Thick, mucus-covered, camouflaged skin has no scales.

Moray Anatomy

Mouth Breathers

In order to breathe, moray eels use organs called **gills**. Gills take in oxygen from water and give off carbon dioxide. After this gas exchange has taken place, a moray squirts the "used" water out of two small openings in the sides of its head.

A moray's gills are very small and cannot take in water on their own. So morays suck water into their mouths. This water then passes over the gills and provides all the oxygen a moray needs.

To suck in water, a moray opens its mouth wide. When the eel has taken in a full "breath" of water, it closes its mouth. Morays must breathe constantly to get the oxygen they need. So these animals are always opening and closing their mouths. For this reason, a resting moray sometimes looks like it is slowly chewing the water. But it is just breathing.

Sensing Its Way

Like all animals, moray eels have senses that help them find their way around. However, although morays have all the same senses as most other animals—sight, hearing, taste, touch, and smell—not all of these senses work very well. Morays have poor eyesight, for instance, and they cannot hear very well, either. Their senses of taste and touch are better, but these senses work best when an object is close by.

The two tubes that extend from the moray's snout help the moray smell its prey.

A moray's sense of smell, however, is very good even at a distance. So a moray depends mostly on this sense. To smell, a moray draws in water through its two front nostrils, which are short tubes that stick up from its snout. Inside the nostrils, nerves gather scent information from the water and send it to the brain. The brain receives this information and decides what the scent means—whether the scent comes from a wounded fish that might make a nice meal or from another moray, for instance. The "used" water then passes out of the moray's body through a smaller set of nostrils located above the moray's eyes.

In addition to the usual senses, morays have a special sense that they share with most fish: They can feel movement that is far away. A moray's head has several deep pores called **lateral line organs**. These organs feel movement in the water. The moray's brain then makes sense of the information. One type of movement might come from a wounded fish, for example. A different type might be made by soft corals waving in the ocean currents. Using the information gathered by the lateral line organs, a moray can learn a great deal about its surroundings without moving around.

Day and Night

It makes sense that moray eels depend on senses other than vision. Morays are **nocturnal** animals, which means they are active mostly at night. Vision is not much help at night, but the senses of smell and touch work well regardless of the light conditions.

Moray eels hunt for food at night, preferably when the weather is stormy.

Morays spend their nights moving from place to place and hunting for food. The darker the night, the more active morays become. Morays also seem to prefer rough conditions, although no one has discovered why. A black, stormy night is perfect traveling weather for a moray eel.

When morning arrives, morays slip into cracks or holes and settle down for the day. A moray's resting place is called a lair. Most morays stay out of sight in hidden lairs during the daytime hours. Some do stick their heads out of cracks, but these are just a small part of the eel population. For every moray that shows its face, there are dozens more curled safely out of sight. This is a good thing. Eels play an important role in the coastal waters of the world. A large moray population helps to keep reefs and other shallow-water habitats healthy.

2

Reef Hunters

All moray eels are **carnivores**. This means they eat the flesh of other animals. Most morays live on a diet of fish and small shelled creatures such as crabs and shrimp. They will also eat squid and octopus if they can find and catch them. They will even eat smaller morays from time to time. And a few species of morays, including the chain moray and the zebra moray, prefer hard-shelled animals such as snails, sea urchins, and mussels.

No matter what it eats, a moray eel does not have any trouble finding and killing its prey. It has many tools and tricks that help it to be a skillful hunter.

The easiest way for a moray eel to get food is simply to sit and wait for it. Coral reefs are busy places

A moray tries to snatch its next meal in a school of señorita fish.

with all kinds of animals moving about. If a moray rests with its head sticking out of the reef, fish or other creatures will eventually move within biting distance. When a prey animal gets close enough, a moray lunges forward and grabs its meal.

But staying in one place does not always provide a quick meal. So morays sometimes leave their lairs to hunt for food, usually at night. Hidden by the dark, a moray pokes its slender body into all kinds of nooks and crannies where prey might be hiding. A moray can also put on a burst of speed to catch fish and other quick-moving animals in the open water.

Moray eels are even known to hide and wait for prey to come near. A moray may settle down in a bed of sea grass or another good hiding place and wait for an animal to wander by. When it does, the moray darts out and grabs its meal.

Although morays are skilled **predators**, they do not hunt often. Morays do not have an active lifestyle, so they do not need a lot of food to survive. Scientists believe that most morays leave their lairs to feed only once every three or four days. After it has eaten, a moray returns to its lair to digest its meal.

A Toothy Mouth

To eat their prey, all morays have mouths full of teeth. The shape of the teeth depends on the moray's diet. The few types of moray eels that eat snails, mussels, and other hard-shelled animals have flat teeth that are perfect for crushing the shells of their prey. Most morays, however, eat softer prey such as fish, squid, and octopus. These morays have mouths full of sharp, needlelike teeth that easily puncture and hold onto wriggling animals.

In sharp-toothed species, the teeth are arranged in rows along the upper and lower jaws. The lower jaw always contains two rows of teeth (one row on each side). In some species, the upper jaw contains two more rows of teeth. In others, it contains three rows of teeth—one row on each side of the jaw plus an extra row down the roof of the mouth. All of the teeth curve back toward the moray's throat. Backward-curving

Inside the wide open mouth of a moray, the sharp teeth curve backward.

teeth grip prey tightly and make it nearly impossible for a moray's meal to escape.

To grab an animal, a moray strikes with its mouth open. When the moray's head reaches the prey, its teeth sink into the prey's flesh. The moray then closes its jaws. As the jaws close, the curved teeth pull back on the prey, forcing it deeper into the moray's mouth.

Eating the Meal

Once a moray eel has caught its prey, it starts to eat it. If the prey is small enough to slide easily down the moray's throat, it is gobbled down whole. Before swallowing, however, the moray may let go of its wounded prey just long enough to get a grip on the animal's head. Animals with hard parts, such as shrimp and fish, are best eaten headfirst to prevent spines and bones from poking the insides of the moray's mouth and throat.

An eel chomps down on the sharp spines of a sea urchin.

If a moray captures an animal that is too big to eat in a single swallow, the animal must be torn into bite-sized pieces. Morays cannot chew, so they tear their prey apart by biting and shaking it. As chunks of flesh come loose, a moray gulps them down one by one until it finishes its meal.

Morays must be careful about the size of the bites they take, though. Because morays breathe by sucking in water through their mouths, food has to be swallowed quickly. A large bite that blocks the mouth for too long could make the moray unable to breathe and cause it to die.

Mortal Enemies

Although moray eels eat many different types of prey, they really seem to enjoy eating octopus. A moray can easily sniff out an octopus that is hiding deep within a coral reef. Then the moray swims into the octopus's home and surprises it by biting deep into the animal's soft body. If it can, the moray starts eating the octopus right away.

Usually, though, finding an octopus is the start of a battle. An octopus is not an easy catch. Octopuses have eight strong arms and a sharp, bony beak that they use to fight predators. To fight off an eel, an octopus may wrap its arms around the head of its attacker and try to pull the moray away. It may also snap at the moray with its beak.

If the octopus is strong enough, it may succeed in pulling the moray away from its body before too

Octopus is a favorite moray meal but catching the octopus is a challenge.

much damage is done. However, the moray has a trick to loosen the octopus's grip. The moray ties its body into a knot near its tail. The moray then works the knot up toward its head. The octopus must let go to avoid getting its arms caught in the knot. With its body free, the moray can continue its attack. If the octopus grabs hold again, the moray just repeats its trick.

When Predator Becomes Prey

Not many animals hunt or eat adult moray eels. Morays are too large and too strong for most reef creatures to tackle. A very few animals, however, do eat morays if they can catch them. Reef-dwelling sharks, for instance, sometimes gobble down a moray eel.

By blending into its surroundings a moray can avoid predators such as sharks.

Groupers, fish that may be thirteen feet long and weigh five hundred pounds, also have been seen eating moray eels. And morays are even in danger from other morays: Large morays sometimes eat smaller ones.

To keep themselves safe from predators, moray eels try to stay hidden. They do this by resting in caves and holes during the day, thus keeping themselves completely out of sight. Most morays also have skin coloring that helps them to fade into the background and avoid being noticed. This type of coloring is called **camouflage**. Many morays even have camouflaged skin inside their mouths. Mouth coloring disguises morays even when they open their mouths to breathe.

Judging by their numbers, morays do a good job of keeping themselves safe. Huge numbers of moray eels roam and hunt the reefs of the world, and it is likely that they will continue to do so far into the future.

chapter 3

The Life of a Moray

Moray eels live long lives. In the wild, morays (especially the larger species) usually reach ten to twenty years of age. These animals can live even longer in aquariums, where there are no predators and little danger of illness or accident. Healthy aquarium morays have been known to live thirty years or more before dying of old age.

During its life, a moray eel moves through a cycle that includes birth, development, adulthood, and parenthood. This cycle produces new moray eels and keeps populations steady.

The Leptocephalus

A moray eel starts its life as a tiny **leptocephalus**. Leptocephali (the plural of leptocephalus) hatch from

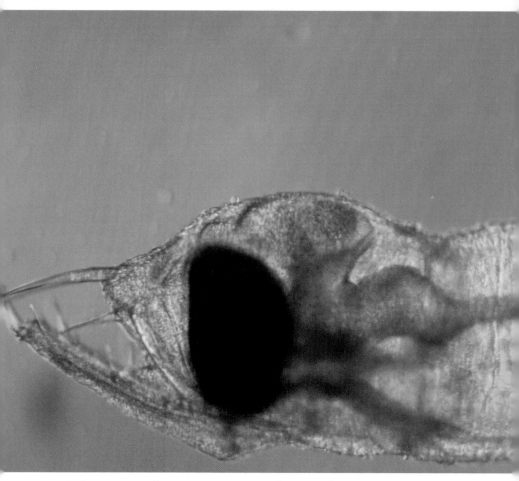

A tiny moray larva as seen under a microscope.

eggs. They have flat, see-through bodies that are shaped like leaves. The young morays look nothing like their adult relatives. They look so different, in fact, that it took scientists hundreds of years to realize leptocephali were eels. Even today, scientists still cannot identify many types of leptocephali. Until a leptocephalus grows into its adult shape, it may be impossible to tell what type of eel it will become.

As soon as a leptocephalus hatches it becomes part of the plankton, a population of tiny plants and animals that floats near the ocean's surface. The leptocephalus swims among the plankton, eating as many tiny creatures as it can catch. If the leptocephalus is a successful hunter, it will catch and eat many creatures, and it will grow bigger and bigger. If the leptocephalus is unlucky, however, it may be caught and eaten by another tiny predator in the plankton, a fish, a whale, or any other animal that eats plankton.

Most leptocephali are unlucky and are eaten within the first few months of their lives. But some continue to live and grow. After six to twelve months in the plankton, a leptocephalus is ready to take the next step in its journey to adulthood.

Becoming an Adult

When a leptocephalus is large enough to survive on its own, it sinks from the plankton. It immediately begins to swim toward the warm, shallow waters that provide good homes for moray eels. When it reaches a comfortable area, the leptocephalus settles to the ocean floor.

After it reaches the bottom, a leptocephalus changes. Its body takes on an adult shape. After this change, the animal is a small adult moray eel. The little eel may take several months to develop its adult coloring, but its body shape is the same as that of a fully grown moray.

Newly hatched morays swim with plankton, which also provides a food source.

The young moray starts living an adult lifestyle right away. It finds a lair and begins searching for food. Morays are solitary animals, which means they live and hunt alone. From the day it adopts its adult shape until the day it dies, a moray eel will keep to itself as much as possible.

Most morays spend their whole lives on the reefs where they first settle. Some morays pick home lairs and establish territories that they defend from intruders. Others change locations often, choosing a new lair every few days. Whatever their habits, however, all of the morays in an area live together peacefully. And most of the time, many different species of morays share the same reef without any trouble.

Though they prefer to be alone, morays can comfortably share lairs after they become adults.

Although the moray is adult in shape as soon as it leaves the leptocephalus stage, it takes the eel a couple of years to reach full maturity. At this point, the eel is ready to reproduce and create the next generation of morays.

Spawning

Moray eels reproduce by **spawning**. This means that females release eggs into the water at the same time that males release sperm into the water. Fertilization happens when the sperm joins with the eggs. The eggs must be fertilized by the sperm in order to begin growing baby moray eels.

Many undersea animals depend on luck to take care of the fertilization process. They are nowhere near each other when they spawn, so ocean currents bring the eggs and sperm together. Moray eels, however, use a different method. A male and a female moray usually swim twisted together while they spawn. Sometimes a female even twists with several males at the same time. By staying close together, the morays give their eggs and sperm a good chance of meeting.

Once spawning is complete, the moray eel's parental responsibilities are over. Moray eels do not take care of their eggs. Instead, they allow the eggs to drift away with the ocean currents. The eggs float near the water's surface until they hatch into leptocephali and start their lives.

There is a lot that scientists do not know about the mating habits of moray eels. They are not sure

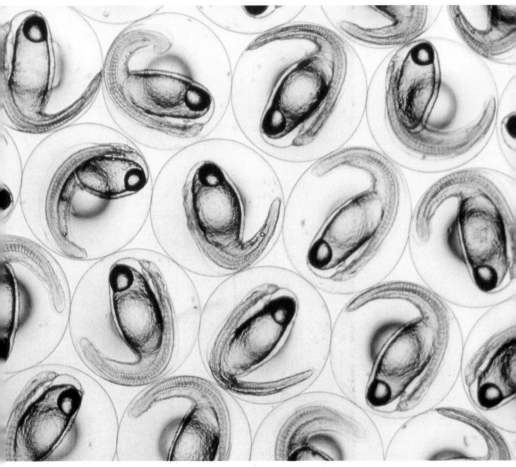

Eel embryos in their eggs, waiting to hatch.

how many eggs morays release, for example, or how often they spawn. Scientists *do* know that morays usually spawn around dusk. They also believe that morays spawn close to home.

Changing Sexes

Nearly all moray species have two sexes: male and female. But there is one exception to this rule, a type of moray called the blue ribbon eel. All blue ribbon

Some blue ribbon eels change from males to females. This helps balance the eel population.

eels start their lives as males. Some, however, change into females later on. This change happens if there are not enough females in the eel population.

The blue ribbon eel is not the only animal that has the ability to change from one sex to another. Many animals, including some fish, shrimp, and frogs, can also do this. Sex change is nature's way of making sure that there are always enough males and females to reproduce and create new generations.

No one knows why blue ribbon eels are the only morays that can change from male to female. But one thing is clear. Even morays without this ability have no trouble keeping their species going. Each year, many millions of new morays move from egg to leptocephalus and from leptocephalus to adult. The cycle of life continues, and the world's moray population stays strong.

4

Understanding Morays

M oray eels have a bad reputation. With their sharp teeth and snakelike bodies, morays look scary. As a result, many people believe that morays are very aggressive animals.

In recent decades, however, scientists have been able to study morays in their underwater homes. As a result, scientists now understand that the moray's scary reputation is undeserved. Most of the time, morays are shy creatures that harm only their intended prey.

Morays are not harmless, however. They can and sometimes do hurt humans. Knowing the facts can help people to enjoy morays without fear, yet treat them with the respect they deserve.

Vicious or Gentle?

Morays are often thought to be aggressive animals that will chase and attack a diver or a snorkeler. This belief is probably due to the moray's open-mouthed breathing technique. Any person who approaches a resting moray will notice that the animal is slowly opening and closing its mouth, showing off its long, sharp teeth. While it does this, the moray keeps its eyes fixed on its human visitor. Between the teeth and the steady gaze, it looks as if the moray is getting ready to attack.

A scuba diver and a friendly moray greet each other.

However, this is not the case. Morays rarely leave their lairs to approach humans, much less attack them. In fact, it is likely that a moray eel will either pull itself farther into its lair or swim away when approached by an underwater intruder. If it can, a moray will nearly always flee rather than fight.

Not only are morays not aggressive, but many even make friends with regular human visitors. In some areas, divers have fed the morays so often that the eels slither out of their lairs in broad daylight whenever people appear. Large green morays are especially well known for this behavior. On popular dive sites in many parts of the world, green morays commonly leave their holes and wrap their slimy bodies around divers, poking their heads here and there in a friendly search for food.

A moray gracefully glides past the hand of a scuba diver as another diver watches.

A Deadly Bite

Many people are afraid not only of being bitten by morays, but also of being poisoned by them. Until recently the moray's bite was said to be deadly to humans. Indeed, long-ago fishermen who caught morays for a living always cut off the heads of their catch. Removing the head was the fishermen's way of avoiding the moray's poisonous fangs.

Today, however, scientists know that moray eels do not have poison in their mouths. This does not mean, though, that a moray's bite is not dangerous. Morays' teeth are covered with germs called bacteria that can make a person sick. The bacteria do not act quickly; it may take several days for a bitten person to become ill. But a wound made by a moray eel can cause all kinds of diseases if it is not cleaned right away.

A moray's bite is also dangerous for another reason. This eel's teeth are needle sharp, and they can shred human flesh. So although a moray's bite is not likely to kill a person, it *is* very painful and can do a lot of damage.

Moray Attacks

Quite a few people have learned this lesson the hard way. Many moray attacks have been recorded, and some of them have been serious.

Most moray attacks occur when divers or snorkelers poke their hands into dark holes in the reef. If a hole happens to contain a moray eel, the swimmer is almost sure to be bitten. The moray is trapped, and it is defending itself in the only way it can.

Some moray attacks also happen when people try to feed eels. But it is likely that these attacks are accidental. Morays have such poor eyesight that they sometimes have trouble seeing where the food ends and the person begins. A moray may lunge forward to grab a tasty piece of fish and find itself with a mouthful of human fingers instead.

Dangerous Food

Even when morays are being eaten rather than doing the eating themselves, they can still be dangerous to people. Moray flesh can cause a type of food poisoning called **ciguatera poisoning**. A mild case of ciguatera poisoning causes nausea, vomiting, and diarrhea. A bad case can cause paralysis or even death.

The ciguatera problem starts with certain types of tiny warm-water plants, called algae, that produce a substance that is poisonous to humans, but not to fish. Small fish and other creatures eat the algae and store the poison in their bodies. Those small fish may be eaten by a moray eel. The eel digests the fish's flesh, but not the poison. The poison is stored in the eel's flesh. As time passes and many meals are eaten, more and more poison builds up in the eel's flesh. For this reason, bigger and older moray eels are more likely to cause ciguatera poisoning than smaller ones.

Although it is possible to become sick from eating moray eels, it is unusual. In many parts of Asia, for example, people eat moray eels as part of their daily diet, and these people almost never experience ciguatera poisoning. This is because eel fishermen understand how to avoid catching poisoned eels. They know, for instance, that large eels should not be sold as food. Fishermen are also careful to catch eels in colder waters, where the algae that cause ciguatera poisoning cannot grow. As long as these easy precautions are taken, morays can be a good and healthy source of food.

Employees at a market in Japan offer eels for sale. Moray eels are a healthy and tasty source of food.

A marine biologist feeds a hungry eel at the Ocean Journey Aquarium in Colorado.

Appreciating the Moray

As science's understanding of moray eels has grown, fear has changed to interest for many people. Today, moray eels are even popular pets. Small species such as zebra morays, snowflake morays, and leopard morays are especially popular for home aquariums.

Whether they are in home tanks or commercial aquariums, captive morays have an important function. They bring part of the ocean world into people's homes and lives. People who might never swim in the ocean can see morays breathe, swim, and eat.

Scuba diving is another window into the moray's world. This sport began in the 1950s and has become more popular over the years. Today, many people dive the world's reefs for fun, relaxation, and education. And these people often see moray eels during their trips under the ocean surface.

Activities like diving and aquarium visits are good for the moray's reputation. By watching and getting to know these animals, people can begin to understand and enjoy moray eels instead of fearing them. And the more people learn about morays, the more the eels will be seen for what they are: beautiful creatures that are an important part of the ocean world.

Glossary

Anguilliformes: The scientific order to which moray eels belong.

camouflage: Skin coloring that helps a moray blend into the background.

carnivore: Any animal that eats only the flesh of other animals.

ciguatera poisoning: A type of food poisoning that is caused by eating the waste products of certain algae.

gills: Organs that release carbon dioxide and take in oxygen.

lateral line organ: An organ that detects and interprets disturbances in the water.

leptocephalus: The name given to a newly hatched moray eel, before it changes into its adult form.

nocturnal: Active mostly at night.

predator: Any animal that hunts and eats other animals to survive.

spawning: Releasing eggs and sperm into the water.

For Further Exploration

Books

Bo Flood, *From the Mouth of the Monster Eel: Stories from Micronesia*. Golden, CO: Fulcrum Publishing, 1996. Eels appear in many legends, including the title story in this book.

Cheryl M. Halton, *Those Amazing Eels*. Minneapolis, MN: Dillon Press, 1990. This book discusses scientific discoveries about eels. It also describes several species of eel, including electric eels and lampreys.

Donald M. Silver, *Coral Reef*. New York: Learning Triangle Press, 1998. Moray eels are part of the coral reef ecosystem. Read about coral reefs and the many animals that live on them in this beautifully illustrated book.

Websites

Scuba Bob Klemow's Moray Eels (www.members. fortunecity.com). This website features a moray eel slide show. See dozens of pictures of morays from all over the world.

The Monterey Bay Aquarium (www.mbayaq.org). This website includes a snowflake moray eel coloring page to print out and color.

Moray Eels (www.enchantedlearning.com). This informational page includes a moray eel drawing to print out and color.

Index

picture credits

about the author

Kris Hirschmann has written more than sixty books for children, mostly on science and nature topics. She is the president of The Wordshop, a business that provides a wide variety of writing and editorial services. She holds a bachelor's degree in psychology from Dartmouth College in Hanover, New Hampshire.

Hirschmann lives just outside of Orlando, Florida, with her husband, Michael.